SRA Open Court Reading

No Way

SRA
A Division of The McGraw-Hill Companies

Columbus, Ohio

www.sra4kids.com

SRA/McGraw-Hill

A Division of The **McGraw·Hill** Companies

Copyright © 2002 by SRA/McGraw-Hill.

All rights reserved. Except as permitted under the United States Copyright Act, no part of this publication may be reproduced or distributed in any form or by any means, or stored in a database or retrieval system, without prior written permission from the publisher.

Printed in the United States of America.

Send all inquiries to:
SRA/McGraw-Hill
8787 Orion Place
Columbus, OH 43240-4027

ISBN 0-07-569756-4

3 4 5 6 7 8 9 DBH 05 04 03 02

"I am in this play," said Ray.
"I am a tree."

"What do you say in the play?" asked Kay.

"I do not say a thing," said Ray.
"A tree may not speak in this play."

"Maybe you can play a trick," said Kay.
"Maybe you can say, *Bark, bark*!"

"A tree may not speak in this play," said Ray.
"But a tree has bark," said Kay.

"No way!" said Ray.
"A tree may not speak in this play."